# The Just Lion

by
Sascha Nieland Allard

George Ronald
Oxford

George Ronald, Publisher
Oxford
www.grbooks.com

2025 by Sascha Nieland Allard

All Rights Reserved

A catalogue record for this book is available
from the British Library

ISBN: 978-0-85398-676-8

Illustrated by Dilmi Amarasinghe

Dedicated to all the children of the world

## The Just Lion

As you take turns playing
beneath the warm summer sun,
you'll see that being fair and just
can make the games more fun.

Luka, the powerful lion,
was feeling grumpy and hot.
He grumbled and he roared,
longing for a cooler spot.

He found a large baobab tree where he could lie on his side, and enjoy the cool shade - with a smile so wide.

Under this protective crown, Luka spent many days, enjoying the lovely relief from the sun's strong rays.

Then, a fruit bat fluttered by.
She said, "Ooh I'd love to stay.
The flowers have sweet nectar,
it would really make my day!"

An elephant arrived next. He said, "I'm parched, you see, and I've heard there's water hidden inside this ancient tree."

Although Luka had found
the baobab first,
he kindly made space for Elephant,
so she could quench her thirst.

Having moved once again
so the elephant could stay,
Luka's legs were in the sun,
during the hottest part of the day.

A monkey soon approached.
"I've been searching for some food -
for branches with hanging fruit.
- I'm so sorry to intrude.

I'd really love to stay -
I hope there's room for me.
I'm very, very hungry -
may I please share your tree?"

Luka shuffled over again,
because he wanted to be fair.
He was barely in the shade,
but happy that his friends were there.

As the blazing sun rose high,
Luka drooped his head.
His body ached, his mane was hot,
his back and cheeks turned red.

But he discovered something else,
much more precious than shade.
Under the special tree's branches,
new friendships had been made.

The tree was not for him alone,
but its shade a gift for all.
With branches wide, it stands to share,
a haven for animals both big and small.

After seeing Luka's sunburn,
his friends said, "but *that* isn't fair."
They wanted to do something
to show their concern and care.

"We'll take turns in the sun",
said the bat with a flap.
"We can all help each other",
said the monkey with a clap.

As they took turns playing beneath the warm summer sun, they found that being fair and just made their games more fun.

Together, they laughed, smiled and played, and Luka said to his friends, "I'd love it if you stayed!"

## Discussion questions

1. What do you think it means to be fair and just?

2. Have you ever seen something unfair and wanted to fix it?

3. Have you ever shared something special with a friend?

4. How did Luka show justice to the other animals?

5. How did the other animals show justice to Luka?

6. How can we help everyone feel happy and included when we play together?

# Collect them all

 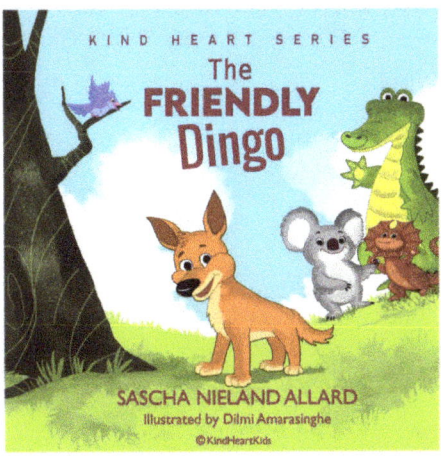 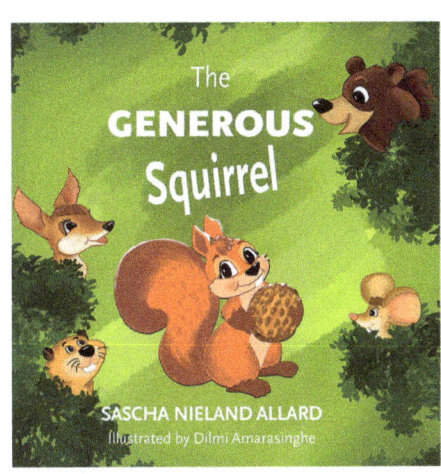

 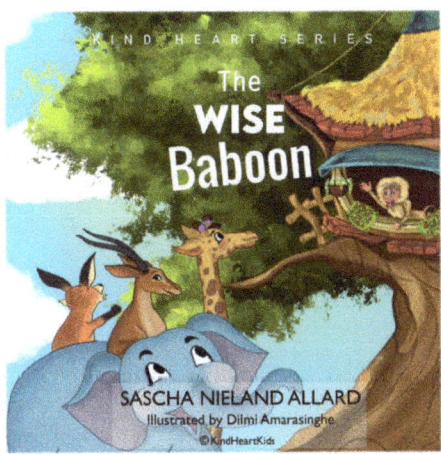 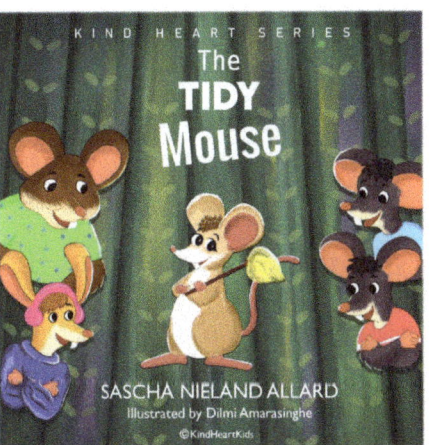

www.kindheartkids.ca

Instagram@Kindheart.kids

www.ingramcontent.com/pod-product-compliance
Lightning Source LLC
LaVergne TN
LVHW070949070426
835507LV00029B/3465